I0157927

Pain and A Powerful God

Edgar (Ted) Stubbersfield

Copyright © 1994 Edgar Stubbersfield

Assigned to Rachel Stubbersfield 2012

All rights reserved.

ISBN: 978-0-9873994-7-2

:

CONTENTS

ACKNOWLEDGMENTS

Pastor Eric Liebeldt, Peace Lutheran Church, Gatton.

For his deep insights on the subject of suffering and the generous use of his library. Yes Eric I often think I am more of a Lutheran than a Pentecostal. May the Lord bless you richly.

Pastor David Steere, Fressingfield Baptist Church, Suffolk

For the trouble you went to in obtaining the out of print book by Anderson, "The Silence of God" I value your friendship and for teaching me that God is indeed omnipotent.

INTRODUCTION

A long time ago I had an uncle who was an active lay preacher in our district. In 1917 he went off to what he thought would be a great adventure, World War One and served with the Desert Column in Palestine and Syria. On his return he never set foot inside a church again. Over the years I still vividly recall his answer when my father asked him why this happened. He told of how, when pursuing the retreating Turks they would ride into village after village only to find the wells, so desperately needed by their horses, filled with the rotting corpses of Armenian Christians who had been mercilessly butchered. He went on to say that he could no longer believe in a God who claims to be loving and powerful yet treated those who serve Him in that way.

This slaughter of the Armenians by the Turks was not an isolated event but part of the first genocide recorded in modern history. Centuries before, Armenia was the first nation to turn, as a people group, to Christianity. to be an Armenian was to be a Christian. The opposition of its Moslem neighbours eventually spilled into open hostility at the end of the nineteenth century and the number of deaths have been estimated at about 1.5 million. The world was outraged by this barbarity. Eventually, in 1895 the Sultan was shamed by world pressure into making a statement attempting to defend the charges of inaction that were hurled against him. The church with its lack of answers at the death of so many believers and missionaries found this a time of great anguish. This despair is echoed in the words of a writer at the time "In vain do we strain our ears to hear some voice from the throne of the Divine Majesty. The far off heaven where, in perfect peace and unutterable glory, God dwells and reigns, is SILENT."[1]

To this day, the real problem for the Christian is not the fact of undeserved suffering but rather the silence of the omnipotent God in the face of it, This silence providing logical "proof" for some that god does not exist.[2] Any Christian worker who has no real answers to the problem of suffering will, like my old uncle, have nothing to offer a questioning world and will even find his faith shipwrecked when his own time of trial comes.

The world has been appalled again with the tragic slaughter in Rwanda continuing as I write. Is all suffering the same? Is there no difference between suffering for being Christians as the Armenians did and the Rwandans, as victims of inter-tribal hatred. When we ask for journeying mercies and we arrive safely we give thanks to our omnipotent God. Should it end in tragedy is that then the work of the devil? How do we counsel a person whose faith has been shaken to its very foundation and will not accept platitudes. These and other difficult but absolutely vital questions will be discussed in this study.

Though I work towards a final conclusion, there are a number of minor conclusions throughout which are intended to aid the

---

[1] Anderson, R. *The Silence of God.* (Pickering & Inglis: London, 9th edition) 5.

[2] This argument runs: Theistic faith claims that God is good, wise and powerful, evils exist that a good, wise and powerful God would not allow, therefore God does not exist.

counsellor. These are in italics. I trust that this small work may help you see, even more clearly, the God of all comfort.

Ted Stubbersfield

19 June, 1994

1. THE OMNIPOTENT GOD

WHAT IS OMNIPOTENCE

The whole problem of the involvement of God in suffering, particularly when a moral cause of that pain is not obvious, is that it can suggest that "God faces some conditions not of his own making."[3] This objection has been answered by the traditional doctrine of God's omnipotence. The word, derived from the Latin *omnipotens*, meaning "all powerful", is used to translate, though not exactly, the Greek *pantokrator* meaning "ruler over all things", which carries with it the connotation of the exercise of that power. This Greek word is in turn a translation through the LXX of the Hebrew for "Lord of Hosts" in Gen 32:1-2. It was originally used by the Hebrews when they were urged, by their leaders, to remember in the day of battle that "they were not to fight as though trusting to their own strength, for then they should have been quickly discouraged at the first reverse in the field. They were to fight in the knowledge that Yahweh, their heavenly ally, was fighting with them and that they were fortunate to have such a powerful deity on their side. Unfortunately, however, their enemy was also equipped with a heavenly ally whose power was not to be underestimated."[4] Through the influence of the prophets a growing understanding of El Shaddai, the all sufficient one became clearer.

---

[3] Mac Gregor, Geddes. *Introduction To Religious Philosophy.* (Macmillan: London, 1972) 287.

[4] Mac Gregor *Introduction...*, 288.

4

The Latin word is found in the earliest creeds and it was first used in a more defined theological manner by Augustine, particularly in his treatise on the Trinity. A simple dictionary definition does not help us, as there are a variety of interpretations of what this all powerfulness actually means. In a real sense, God is not omnipotent. Aquinas argued that the one limitation on God's omnipotence is that He cannot do something that is against his nature, such as commit a sinful act. In this same vein would be an inability to turn past events into future or non existing ones.

Anyone who has witnessed a severe electrical storm, where the sky is lit up across the horizon with sheet lightning combined with the jagged bolts and deafening thunder can only be left with a sense of awe. Yet the power of electricity has been studied and mastered by the scientists and we, in complete safety, can make it work as our slave with the flick of a switch. Such an illustration would seem to fall very far from understanding God's omnipotence, yet it is gaining popularity in the health and wealth doctrines of teachers like Kenneth Hagin and Kenneth Copeland. "Hagin claims through the discovery of the "spiritual laws" established by God to run the universe, the believer can put these laws to "work" for his own use."[5] He teaches that since the "law of faith is impersonal, just like the law of gravity, it works regardless of who the person is, or where he or she stands with Christ."[6] This turns the Almighty from a sovereign to a subject, from a person to a principle and removes the moral issue of undeserved suffering.

This teaching is threatening to tear the Pentecostal church down the middle, many responsible leaders seeing such a view of God's

---

[5] Mc Connell, D. *The Promise of Health and Wealth.* (Hodder & Stoughton: Sevenoaks, 1990) 135.

[6] Mc Connell *Promise...,*136.

omnipotence as sub Christian. They point to a trail of ruined lives for, when suffering comes, men find that God cannot be commanded. This bring them into condemnation for having insufficient faith. Rather than taking issue with God the problem is perceived as a failing in themselves.[7]

Understanding what omnipotence is not, what then is it? As we have seen, God's omnipotence is not to be seen as a total power to do anything. He cannot make a square circle and it is exercised within the bounds of his nature. It cannot be manipulated like some impersonal force. Omnipotence may be defined as "that by which God independently, through the eternal activity of his own essence, can do absolutely everything that does not involve a contradiction."[8] This characteristic of God cannot be separated from his other natures. Assume for instance that God was not omniscient, we could argue that though God means well and knows far more than myself, he could have overlooked something in the demands he makes of me. Most importantly it cannot be separated either from his justice and goodness.

Omnisapience is the attribute of God whereby he is all wise, the key to justice, and this has been defined as "the accurate judgement of God, by which he knows how to dispose and ordain all causes and effects in a most admirable manner for the attainment of His end, Job 12, 13, 28, 20, Rom 11:33, (and is) beyond the reach of

---

[7] This approach to God's omnipotence is one the writer has had to face on many occasions when counselling people who have faced long term suffering.

[8] Schmidt, H. *Doctrinal Theology Of The Evangelical Lutheran Church.* (Augsburg Publishing House: Minneapolis, 1961) 120.

human and angelic judgement"[9] In every issue where there is an apparent lack of justice the Biblical God has been aware of the situation, passed a perfect judgement and allowed the situation to continue. God's goodness is said to be two fold. Firstly he possesses it *absolutely* "because he contains within himself all perfections (Matt 5:48; Lk 18:19)".[10] And, secondly, *respectively* "or in relation to creatures to whom God is good since He efficiently produces every created good (Acts 17:25, 28; Jam 1:17; 1 Cor 4:7) and this according to his own perfection, as the ideal or pattern of created perfection; and it attracts also, and excites to the love and desire of himself as the chief good."[11] This second form of goodness is better known as holiness

The problem for the counsellor in the face of undeserved suffering is that he is dealing with a situation that God knew about, had complete power to alter yet in his perfect wisdom and goodness has allowed. If a questioner proceeds along these lines these facts must be acknowledged. Because God's natures are so intermingled a denial of his justice and/or goodness is in effect a denial of God's omnipotence.

OMNIPOTENCE AND THE PROBLEM OF SUFFERING

Without an omnipotent, omniscient, omnipresent and omnisapient God we ultimately do not have a problem, Christianity has rightly rejected this approach attacking the problem face on.

---

[9] Schmidt *Theology...*, 120.

[10] Schmidt *Theology...*, 120.

[11] Schmidt *Theology...*, 120-1.

For the deist, the question of the goodness and justice of God does not occur. God, they maintain, created the world then stood back from it as his creation ran like clockwork through the laws he ordained. This is not the Biblical picture of God's care for his creation. The Old Testament abounds with a long history of the divine intervention of the omnipotent in the events of man and when our Lord dwelt among us His ministry was full of the miraculous. "Just as any man who is possessed of the means and the opportunity to relieve suffering is impelled to action by his very nature so it was with our blessed Lord."[12] These could not be separated from his teaching ministry but were an integral part of it. These were not just any miracles "but they were such miracles as the Jews were led by their Scriptures to expect"[13], Dt 18:15. This was a time when none were turned away and it appeared that wrongs would be righted and sorrow give way to peace and happiness.

The early promise of Jesus was continued with the ministry of the Apostles through whose ministry a suffering world would see greater (at least numerically) blessings than were performed by the master. Chains fell off prisoners, houses shook through prayer, yet, at a time when the church was facing the philosophy and civilisation of the gentile world, the miraculous passed away. Anderson repeats the cry of many who experience suffering when he writes "The mystery remains that God who at sundry times and in diverse manners spake in time past unto the fathers never speaks to his people now! The divine history of the favoured race for thousands of years teems with miracles by which God gave proof

---

[12] Anderson *Silence...*,.39.

[13] Anderson *Silence...*, 41.

of his power with men, and yet we are confronted with the astonishing fact that from the days of the apostles to the present hour the history of Christendom will be searched in vain for the record of a single public event to compel belief that there is a God at all!"[14] He voices the conclusion of many when he says "In the presence of the stern and dismal facts of life, the faith of earlier days gives way, for surely a God who is entirely passive and always unavailable is for all practical purposes nonexistent.[15]

The most difficult task for a counsellor in the face of undeserved suffering is to make a silent God relevant and his task is not made any the easier when the questioner points to the miracles in the scripture and questions why, with the same faith, do the same miracles not happen again? The counsellor must not be quick to suggest that the answer lies in a lack of faith in the questioner, nor blame the suffering on a second party, Psm 66:10-12; Job 1:21.

---

[14] Anderson *Silence...*, 18. I would not go quite as far as Anderson but accept the general principal.

[15] Anderson *Silence...*, 10.

FINDING THE OMNIPOTENT GOD

THE DRY GULLY OF REASON

The problem of suffering is only a problem if God is, in fact, omnipotent, a viewpoint that has not always been universally held. Cicero's apology for Jupiter's neglect of the world was that "the sovereign of the universe is on the whole a good sovereign, but with so much business on his hands that he has not time to look into details.[16] This less than omnipotent God is not worthy of our worship but probably still reflects the vague thoughts of many people, even Christians, today. This defective view of God's omnipotence can be an outworking of petitionary prayer, where through pleading hard enough, a Christian believes he can gain God's attention and attain a priority in his busy schedule.

Two thousand years after Cicero, much the same view is still propounded by some with the belief philosophers have termed as the "metaphysical lack" in God's creation and thus ultimately in God himself. Here God's power is likened to a ray of sunshine that diminishes in intensity the further it travels from its source. This neoplatonic position was brought into Christianity through the writings of Augustine and Aquinas.

This view of God's power is far from the one presented by the Bible, which, from its opening verses, presents him as creating the universe from nothing. Throughout its ensuing pages the affairs

---

[16] Anderson *Silence...*, 61.

and imagination of men and empires are said to be totally in the control of the Almighty. Its concluding pages claim that the universe, which owes its sustenance to him, will be bought to a climatic close when all will be judged. Far from being too busy to care about details, not the slightest detail escapes his notice.

The self attestation of scripture to itself and the omnipotent God revealed in its pages is insufficient for some who seek, through reason, a basis for their faith. These arguments fall into three categories listed below

1. *A posteriori* Where only the existence of God can account for some aspect of the universe.

2. *A priori* There is something about man that gives a clue to the existence of God.

3. *Revelational* Where God makes himself known to man in a totally convincing way.

If these proofs are valid they provide compelling ground for a belief in God and from which could be argued his attributes. They would buttress faith, ultimately silencing doubts that assail in the face of suffering.

The Roman Catholic Church has taught that the existence of God can be demonstrated by natural reason through the *a posteriori* proofs.[17] As recently as 1950 Pope Pius 12 pronounced in his

---

[17] In 1835 Abbe Bautain was forced to recant his belief that God is known by faith alone and acknowledge that his existence can be demonstrated by natural

encyclical *Humani Generis* that "human reason ... by its natural powers and light can in fact arrive at true and certain knowledge of one personal God who in his providence guards and directs the world and also the natural law infused into our souls by the creator." This was reiterated in Vatican 1 "that God, the beginning and end of all things, can be known with certitude by the natural light of human reason from created things".[18]

These proofs found their clearest expression in the five proofs of Thomas Aquinas.[19] Though they refused to die, the authority given to these arguments was destroyed by William of Ockham when he posed the question "Does pushing back the cause-effect sequence to a prime mover really prove the existence of an Ultimate Being, namely the God of the Bible, or merely an adequate cause which might be a limited power or being but less than God himself?"[20] This question aptly carries the name "Ockham's razor.". During the enlightenment Thomas' proofs were turned against the church as it was rightly pointed out that even if accepted, they said nothing, good or bad, about God's nature except that he designs.

---

reason. Lutheran theologians from Melanchthon up to Kierkegaard, through the use of Aristotelian Philosophy could "prove" creation ex nihilo, the resurrection of the body and the trinity. Such exulted claims were made for reason and philosophy that it would appear that there was little remaining for revelation and faith.

[18] Schwarz, H. *The Search For God.* (Augsburg: Min. 1975) P. 58.

[19] These are 1. *Motion,* God is the prime mover but not moved, 2. *Causation,* i.e. the cosmological argument where god is the uncaused cause, 3. *Possibility and Necessity*, God is absolutely independent, 4. *Graduation of being*, God is perfectly developed and 5. *Governance of the world*, i.e. the teleological argument, God gives the world its pattern.

[20] Menzies, W. *Apologetics.* (ICI: Brussels, 1988) 61.

Many have spoken of a restlessness in man, such as a longing for truth, an awareness of his own finitude and a need for blessedness. Augustine in the opening of his *Confessions* reflected on man's relation to God, "thou hast made us for thyself and restless in our heart until it comes to rest in thee".[21] These are all examples of *a priori* arguments. Other arguments in this category are the ontological, moral and aesthetic arguments. While many relate to the reasoning behind these arguments they are ultimately unverifiable.

Ultimately the arguments from reason cannot substitute for, or validate faith. The arguments have value but only as a pointer to God, taking us no further than the words of Cicero quoted above, Some will allow that it may take us to the point where our unaided mind can acknowledge that God is but never what God is. Ultimately a man, if he wishes to proceed past raw emotion, must make the commitment to either faith or unbelief. If the decision is for faith, these pointers then authenticate and strengthen that faith.

In the *revelational* argument the traditional proofs are discarded and instead of man trying to prove that God exists, God himself proves his own existence. This is done through the proclamation of the Gospel and the experience is self authenticating. The diversity of the mystical religious experience show the danger of using the experience as the proof itself.

---

[21] Augustine. *Confessions*. Book 1, Chapter 1.

The question of whether God is in fact omnipotent is not influenced in any way by our faith or unbelief, our response only having a bearing on the amount of culpability we correctly or incorrectly lay at God's feet in the face of suffering. If there is no acknowledgment of an omnipotent God the problem, at least to the person involved, ceases to lose its moral significance and simply becomes an unfortunate fact. If God's existence and omnipotence are acknowledged, and this can only be done through faith in the self attestation of scripture, then the dilemma becomes so great as to question the soundness of that step of faith. A belief that God is less than omnipotent at least would make it easier to believe in the goodness of God.

Once the step from reason and raw emotion to faith has been made, suffering can be looked at in a different light. It then becomes difficult if not impossible for the sufferers or witnesses "to give a criterion or criteria whereby they would give up their belief in God no matter what the conditions"[22] This is not to say that faith is not held in tension with the facts but that the facts need not overcome the faith. The counsellor firstly needs to determine if the questioner has indeed made the "leap of faith".

---

[22] Ramm, B. *A Christian Appeal to Reason.* (ICI: Brussels, 1988) 97.

2. DOUBT – A BIBLICAL PERSPECTIVE

INTRODUCTION

Faith and doubt are seen as the antithesis of each other, Mt 14:31, 21:21; Mk 11.23; 1 Tim 2:8, so much so that it would be easy to envisage the Christian faith as something always lived at a high plateau. Such an outworking of faith has seldom been reflected in the experiences of the saints in the face of suffering. Faith is always seen as something that is tried and tested.

Running through both the Old and New Testaments is the theme of victorious faith which had been perfected by suffering, 2 Cor 5:2; Heb 11:36-38; 1 Pet 1:7, 4:2, e.g. Noah for 100 years as he built the ark; Abraham for 20 years as he waited for the promised birth of his son Isaac and later when he was commanded to sacrifice Isaac on Mount Moriah or the New Testament saints in the face of persecution. This trial of faith is not seen as some light matter but capable of attacking the very foundations of faith itself, so much so that we are specifically taught in the Lord's Prayer to petition God that it may not come our way, Mat 6:13. Some, nevertheless, do face this testing but those who do are assured that in passing through it there is great blessing at the other side, James 1:2,12. James does not speak of a masochistic pleasure[23] in suffering itself but urges the believers to look past their present situation and focus on the blessing ahead, the same as with the unpleasant experience of childbirth. This result of testing is not seen as automatic, the

---

[23] Melina, a great Roman lady lost her husband and two of her three sons in one week. Her reaction was to thank God: "More easily can I serve thee, O Lord in that thou hast relieved me of so great a burden".

suffering rather carrying with it the potential both to purify and to corrupt. There can be no testing of the faith without temptation to, or even actual, doubt. This process of holding faith and doubt at the same time is probably the most devastating experience a Christian can pass through. How can he respond to this?

FAITH IN FAITH ITSELF

The hyperfaith movement would maintain that to hold this tension is the worst possible sin short of sinning against the Holy Spirit. The positive confession school talks as much about the power of negative confession as much as it does of positive confession. Doubt is seen as a creative force hindering a Positive Mental Attitude, the fount from which all positive confession flows. Hagin says "What we believe is a result of our thinking, if we think wrong we will believe wrong ... if we believe wrong, our confession will be wrong. In other words what we say will be wrong and it will all hinge on our thinking".[24] Faith in faith has replaced faith in God. This teaching leaves no place for importunate prayer, Mt 6:11; Ja 1:5; Lk 11:3.

With this teaching the plain facts are denied and in reference to healing, Hagin again says "real faith in God - heart faith - believes the Word of God regardless of what the physical evidences may be" and that "a person seeking healing should look to God's Word and not his symptoms"[25] With this teaching, doubt can never really be dealt with as it must never be acknowledged. Regrettably,

---

[24] McConnell *Promise..,* 138, citing Hagin, "Right and Wrong Thinking" 3.

[25] McConnell *Promise..,* 152, citing Hagin, "Real Faith" P.13.

despite its origins in the metaphysical cults this teaching has gained popularity in Pentecostal and Charismatic churches.[26] "Spiritual honesty and moral integrity have been unfortunately replaced by an unrealistic and saccharine piety which is untrue to life".[27] We will see below a different response from the Old Testament saints.

SOME BIBLICAL EXAMPLES

JOB

Job is presented from the very outset as an Old Testament saint without peer, 1:8, 2:3, yet following the accusation by Satan that he only served God from self interest, 1:9, the Almighty allows the accuser to inflict great suffering on his saint, 1:12, 2:6. In a short space of time this rich man with a large family loses his wealth, his family and his own health and, covered with boils, he sits in the dust. He knows that God has hidden His face from him and his wife urges him to "curse god and die", 2:9. His cry is not "why does God *permit* me to suffer these things but why does God *make* me suffer these things,[28] 7:20-21, 9:32-35. He ponders how his sufferings are compatible with his Godhead, 10:2, 19:7."

---

[26] This has been ably demonstrated in McConnell's work cited above. The thoughtfully written " the Believer and Positive Confession" published by the Assembly of God (Gospel Publishing House: Springfield, 1980) should be consulted for a concise and balanced view of what the Pentecostal position should be on this teaching.

[27] Ramm *Christian...,* 140.

[28] Buber, M. A God Who Hides His Face, in Nahum N. Glatzer editor *The Dimensions of Job*, (Schocken" New York, 1969) 57.

Four explanations are offered in this book as the reason for his suffering. The first is as a result of "God allowing a creature, who wanders about the earth, and is subject to him in some way, the Satan, that is the "Hinderer" or "Adversary", to entice him."[29] In this view, God's actions are questioned far more than Job's. This understanding is still held by many Christians who place a large emphasis on demonic activity in the world and the accusations made by some against God's goodness would be well placed if this view was the whole understanding of Job.

The second view, presented by Job's miserable comforters is that punishment follows unrepentant sin, 15:1-6, 20:4-6. That view is still extremely common in both the church and the world. There is no indication in the book of Job that we are to see the avenging hand of God in all suffering. Had it been present it would have made God reasonable and rational even to the mind of unregenerate men. While at time the friends were profound, their viewpoint was narrow, forcing the realities of life into their religious theories, refusing to come to terms with the radical problem they faced. Their viewpoint would allow men to cling strongly to God's justice but strip the unfortunate Job of honour.

Job's own view is that though he does not regard himself as sinless, 7:20, 14:16ff, his sufferings are not commensurate with his sin. Job had believed God to be just but because of his sufferings can no longer hold that view, 9:22. Yet his faith is not totally broken down. It is "no longer possible for one who has been smitten with such sufferings to think God just. "It is all one - Therefore I say:

---

[29] Buber *God...*, 58.

He destroyeth the innocent and the wicked".[30] Yet while it would not seem correct to follow God, Job still retains his faith. Earlier he had a single faith in God and in justice but "he believes now in justice in spite of believing in God and he believes in God in spite of believing in justice. But he cannot forgo his claim that they will be united somewhere, sometime, although he has no idea in his mind how this will be achieved",[31] 19:25-27. This will be closer to the view of Christians who have ever questioned.

After each had said his part, God spoke to Job in Chapters 38-41 but He did not give any reasons for His actions. In these chapters God questioned Job about his understanding of natural phenomenon and Job had to admit that he did not understand them. If Job could not understand the creation with which he has immediate contact and by which he eats, lives and breathes he must be even more at a loss to understand the secret providences of God where He cares for man's spiritual and eternal wellbeing. If Job can trust God in creation without understanding it should he not also trust him in providence? Job "learns that he may well trust God in the mysteries of evil, for he has learned to trust God and his goodness and wisdom in the clarities of creation."[32]

When God appeared there was no indictment as Job's friends expected but Job was not blameless and was accused by God, through his questioning, of confusing the issue by speaking without knowledge. Job in his heresy is not even asked to repent. There is a similarity between the speeches of God and those of his

---

[30] Buber *God...*, 60.

[31] Buber *God...*, 60.

[32] Ramm *Christian...*, 269.

comforters, with the emphasis on the power of God and Job's insignificance and also that he was presumptuous in criticising God. His friends differed in that they had added to it the offensive and untrue contention that Job was wicked while never trying to help Job or strengthen him in his God. Instead they tried to "break down his spirit and coerce him into acting dishonestly in denying the plain facts of experience to support their creed",[33] 13:7-8.

Job certainly was not right in concluding so quickly that God was unjust but God showed that he was "better pleased with honest heresy than with fraudulent piety; and although the outworks of his faith were sorely shaken, his ultimate faith in God weathered the storm triumphantly".[34] His doubt came not as a result of a settled attitude of rebellion and unbelief but from a despair that trembled on the brink of suicide, 7:21. Job's own faith developed through his journey along the road of doubt. This faith appears originally to be motivated by fear, 3:25, and an overscrupulous conscience but through his suffering and loss of his first "faith" he would come to an intimacy not previously experienced. Through it he would come to see God with his eyes rather than previously only hearing about him, 42:5.

There are no answers in Job as to why these sufferings occurred but it stands testimony that faith can remain intact and strengthened through the path of pain and suffering.

---

[33] Pollock, S. God and a Heretic in Nahum N Glatzer editor *The Dimensions of Job*. (Schocken: New York, 1969) 268.

[34] Pollock *God...,* 270.

PSALM 73

The problem posed by the righteous suffering has a corollary in the question "Why do the wicked prosper?" and Psalm 73 explores that question. In this Psalm the writer complains that God is indifferent to injustice and suffering and that the piety of a good man is a mockery. As he faces injustice head on he is confused, a theme common to many Psalms, but he is so confused by it that he almost stumbled and slipped, v2.

In verses 4-11 he describes the different types of prosperity that the wicked enjoy and how they never seem to experience God's judgement. They arrogantly assert "How can God know? Is there knowledge in the most high"? The Psalmist is totally confused about the purpose of his own piety and as to what he should tell his children concerning the value of serving God.

In verse 17 we read that he went to the sanctuary and there things changed when he saw the situation as it should have been viewed. "in the sanctuary, hearing by whatever means the Word of God, he saw the situation from the perspective of divine revelation".[35] The psalmist admits that he had become bitter towards God, v21 because his thinking was little better than an animal's, v22. He understands through God's revelation that the prosperity of the wicked is only apparent and not real and that though he is now inactive he will not always remain so. The writer comes to understand that piety will be one day rewarded.

---

[35] Ramm *Christian...*, 139.

The doubt that the Psalmist experienced is the same as that of Job's for both men were too quick in their imputation of a lack of justice and goodness to God. Also that trust returned when they both regained their spiritual perspective through an encounter with God Himself or His word. Divine revelation is what is needed to regain perspective.

THE GOD WHO HIDES HIS FACE

The Scriptures place such a significance on God's revelation of himself in dealing with pain and suffering and finding in him, if not the answer, at least the trust necessary. What then happens when God, as it were, hides his face at such a time? The *Dues Absconditus*, the God who hides his face, has already been touched on in our sections on Job and Psalm 73 and an understanding of this issue is critical for any counsellor facing the issue of suffering for, it deals with *why* those suffering may find it difficult to trust God. This issue has two distinct sides, the first is when the Almighty hides his face from the unbeliever and the second when he hides from the believer.

This is such a universal problem that even our Lord on the cross cried, "My God, My God, Why have you forsaken me?" Job also "cries: "Why"? The reason is that Job makes the terrible and disappointing discovery that there seems to be a paradox in God himself. God makes no sense to him, God has created him and preserved him, only evidently to destroy him, c.f. Job 10:8 & 18."[36] This response is the opposite to that of the Stoics who would

---

[36] Hebart, S.P. *Lutheran Dogmatics.* (Undated Lecture notes) 28.

accept their fate with calm and resignation. "Why?" can be a cry of faith, not unbelief.

For many it is out of the pain, suffering and utter pointlessness of suffering that the quest for God is born. The quest is not the answer, nor is its commencement the guarantee of its completion but the quest does show us a God we do not know, Gen 32:24ff;1 King 19:4: Job 3:11; Mk 14:32ff; Acts 17:22ff; Rom 1:20ff. As the unbeliever pursues the quest he becomes aware that the God he is seeking brings with him both compulsion and obligation. This particularly happens when the seeker acknowledges restrictions in the moral field and is compelled to act in certain ways. This poses even greater problems for "if we acknowledge an obligation to the full, then clearly we must carry it out to the full. Unfortunately, however, there is for this moral purpose only a very limited moral self at our disposal ... bringing the seeker into greater tension with the God he is trying to find because he cannot fulfil his obligation."[37]

The quest can only leave a man "certain that we are the targets for his attacks, although He created us, and this attack is directed against us in our totality involving every sphere of existence. What He intends for us, we do not know; why He finally kills us, we do not know; why He imposes demands upon us without giving us the ability to fulfil them, we do not know. So the quest for God ends in the utter darkness of complete senselessness where we hear only the empty echoes of our cry, "Why?", and where there is no answer."[38] But where reason ends, faith starts and the *Dues*

---

[37] Hebart *Lutheran...*, 28.

[38] Hebart *Lutheran...*, 30.

Arevelatus, the God who reveals himself, becomes known.

The problem for the believer is very different. Clearly, God does withdraw himself in the face of unrepentant sin but this is not the issue. I am referring to someone who has passed through the stage of seeking and has known the imminence of the God who reveals himself, has maintained a faithful Christian walk yet finds that this same God, who has promised to never forsake him, has withdrawn. This is the reason for the complaints of Job and the psalmist and of our Lord Himself. What is a believer to understand when in the face of suffering, instead of passing through this period cocooned in God's love and grace, as most likely he had previously, it appears that the heavens are as brass and that he is alone?.

The most immediate response is that of doubt, doubt about the believer and about God himself. For the believer, he questions himself deeply, what secret sin have he may have committed that God has abandoned him and whether, in fact, his knowledge of God was only an illusion. He can easily, at this time, question the goodness and justice of the Omnipotent. The book of Job clearly teaches that these times can occur and can strike at the very core of faith itself.

This is a period of great tension between faith and doubt as believing faith is the gift of God. Should he withdraw to any measure that faith, our constancy is difficult, if not impossible, to maintain. From the book of Job we see that a believer can know with certainty that this withdrawal is not as a result of personal sin but that it is God who appears to have moved. He can also intuitively know that, despite what his senses tell him, there is more to the situation than meets the eye. He can also know that God's justice and goodness, although apparently absent will one day be reconciled. He can also believe that somewhere, somehow there will be a reconciliation and vindication. He can also be assured that there will be few that understand and encourage him to remain faithful.

The popular poem, *Footprints*, graphically illustrates how this withdrawal is more to do with our perception of reality than reality itself. This withdrawal is not to be seen as a punishment, but a privilege reserved for those especially loved by God, as in passing through it the believer will be baptised into His love and compassion and enters a new and deeper relationship. As with the unbeliever so also for the believer the discovery of the *Dues Absconditus* is meant to be the start of a search for God, this time through faith, not reason and intended to reach a higher plateau of faith than previously reached   When John the Baptist was imprisoned and his faith shaken we observe that "when John said his worst about Jesus, Jesus said His best about John".[39] Martin Luther, a man who knew much rejection himself, preached on Jesus' rejection of the Canaanite woman and his calling her a dog on no less than 13 occasions. He commented "this is the hardest text of all, to be called a dog"[40] what faith rose in her when, in spite of apparent rejection she would not give up her search and found in the "No", the "Yes" of God who did accept her.   Such experiences, Luther claimed, were the anvil on which all true theology was forged

---

[39] Graham, B. *Till Armageddon.* (Hodder & Stoughton: Sevenoaks, 1981) 31 quoting Vance Havner, source unknown.

[40] Tidball, D. *Skilful Shepherds.* (IVP: Leicester, 1986) 182.

Jesus experienced this *Dues Adsconditus* as he hung on the cross and cried, "My God, My God, why hast thou forsaken me?" Yet knowing he was deserted by his Father he would not accept his deserted state. In faith he pursued after his father committing his forsaken soul, even in the grips of hell, to the Father's keeping. On the third day his Father reversed the verdict of ungodly men and the stone was rolled away, Acts 2:23-24. God had proved himself trustworthy, His son was promised and was given, nothing was held back, no humiliation, no pain, no suffering. When the Christian feels the grip of despair, sensing God's desertion, he needs to know that however things may appear he will never need to cry Eloi, Eloi, lama Sabachthani, Mt. 27:46. The believer must, like the Son, continue to commit himself to the grace and love of the still immanent God. He has promised never to forsake us and he has proven himself trustworthy

The counsellor, when dealing with the deep hurts carried by a questioner, must examine why that person doubts the goodness and power of God. If he is still on the search for the God who has hidden his face he must urge him to respond in faith to God, as outside of faith God will always remain hidden. As for the believer, the counsellor must be very slow to judge his doubt as it can be flowing from the deepest despair caused by God's hand on him in a powerful yet terrible way. The counsellor must remember that "if Job was humbled by his experience, the friends were humiliated. They were condemned for having falsifying facts in the defence of the character of God, and we are afforded the edifying spectacle of the heretic, Job being commanded to pray for his eminently orthodox friends. "[41]

---

[41] Pollock *God...*, 271.

3. SUFFERING – A BIBLICAL PERSPECTIVE

INTRODUCTION

People frequently refer to "undeserved suffering", which suggests that all suffering is not the same. Indeed, there are many factors that come to bear in the consideration of suffering. My father in law was hospitalised with a shrapnel wound when fighting in Italy during World War 2, a common enough occurrence in any conflict. What is surprising is that he was not aware that he was carrying such a serious wound for two weeks, his mind being taken up with the intensity of the battle. Apparently this is not an uncommon occurrence and illustrates graphically that suffering can never be divorced from its circumstances and the importance given to it by its recipient.

The scripture sees all suffering as an intervention into the affairs of men, at the beginning it was not so. The scene in the garden is pictured as idyllic and the closing pages see suffering again absent. Its entry is said to be the result of wilful rebellion against the Creator, Gen 3. To deny its present existence, as the metaphysical cults do is a crime against reason and God who wills that we come to terms with the existence of pain and suffering in his purposes.

Suffering in the New Testament is of three separate types which we will look at below.

SIN PAIN

There are times when sin and suffering can be directly linked, but this link covers the whole spectrum of human piety and can be graphically illustrated by looking at its two extremes. The first and most obvious is as a consequence of breaking an agreed moral standard, as when a bank robber is shot in the process of committing his felony. The other extreme is as an outworking of a misdirected piety as when people die of starvation in Calcutta while sacred cows wander the streets unharmed or closer to home the self flagellation of the monks of old. The connection is not always so obvious but a link can be established none the less, an example of direct suffering as in the case of delayed damage done to the body following years of substance abuse even if that abuse has stopped. This type of pain is not within the scope of this study.[42] Our study will be limited to pain where there is no apparent, even if distant cause and effect.

The examples of Noah, Sodom and Gomorrah, Ananias and Sapphira and Herod teach clearly that God does judge sinfulness, but his hand is not always as clearly seen, nor can it always be interpreted as such. The book of Job teaches clearly that we must be very slow to assume a link between sinful actions and pain unless there is very clear evidence of it. Much harm is done by counsellors who wish to establish a nonexistent link between sin and suffering.

---

[42] Some would disagree and see our hapless bank robber or Calcutta beggar as the innocent victims of their environment.

HUMAN PAIN

This may be described as "suffering which comes because you are human, not related to any specific sin, but to sinfulness, (it encompasses) any kind of hardship or stress common to mankind (and) sickness and suffering that comes *in spite* of your Christianity".[43] A variety of words are used to describe this type of suffering as shown in the table below

WORD	REFERENCE	MEANING
Mastix	Mk 5.29	whip, lash, torment, suffering
Kline	Rev 2.22	bed, couch, sickbed
Thlipsis	Rev 2.22	suffer intensely
Basanismos	Rev 9.5	torture
Basanos	Mt. 4.24	torture, suffering
Kakos echein	Mt. 4.24	illness
Kakos daimonidzetai	Mt 15.22	demon possession
Sunechomene pureto Megalo	Lk 4.38	suffering a high fever
Hudropikos	Lk 14.2	suffering from dropsy

Human pain is not seen as anything more than an unfortunate fact of present human existence, its presence saying nothing about the

---

[43] From an untitled and undated study by Aub Podlich.

goodness or otherwise of the recipient. Jesus clearly taught, Luke 13:1-5, that this type of suffering befalls the godly and ungodly alike and carries with it no particular virtue or stigma. This pain, though an outworking of the sinful and fallen nature of creation, is still an area in which God's grace can be manifested and his love for the sufferer manifested. The merit that may come with this pain is not attached to the experience of suffering itself but the way that faith is brought to bear in the situation, the same as in every other event in life.

While acknowledging that most times there is not a link between sinful actions and suffering, does any man suffer unjustly? Is he born with a clean slate or steeped in sin? Or, if forgiven all, does he now no longer sin through a second work of grace? Those that deny original sin[44] must have great problems with the matter of suffering for often, as in the case of an "innocent" child, the goodness of God must be called into question. Biblical theology, though not detracting from the tragedy of human suffering, sees no man suffering as innocent. This guilt carried by all men is twofold, it is *imputational*, Rom 5:9, flowing from the original sin of Adam and imputed to us in the same way that Christ's righteousness is imputed to us. Also this guilt is ours by *natural regeneration*, whereby the original sin has given rise to a deep corruption in man.

---

[44] The belief that we are created with a clean slate, was not only the view of the English philosophers but also a theological view promoted by the heretic Pelagius. His view is based on Ez18:20, The sons shall not bear the iniquity of the father, Jn 4:11, Rom 9:11. Infants are pronounced innocent, Rom 4:15. Where there is no law there is no transgression & how do godly parents propagate ungodly children. These are all matters that are easily dealt with in scripture. Sadly this heresy appears to be gaining more acceptance in my own denomination. Scriptures in support of original sin are Gen 6:5, 8:21; Job 14:4; Ps 14:2-3, 58:3; Isaiah 48:8, Jn 3:5; Eph 2:3; and especially Psm 51:5; Rom 5:12-14 Gen 5:3.

The human suffering of those in the holiness movements who now consider themselves sinless must also pose great problems. Such people seeing themselves as innocent deceive themselves, 1 Jn 1:8. Tragically the world in much of its discussion on suffering deceives itself, not aware of its fallen state and that it deserves no different fate from that of the antediluvian world.

KINGDOM PAIN

THE SUFFERING OF CHRIST

In view of the great diversity of words used for human pain it is very significant that invariably when Christ's suffering is spoken of, either by himself or others, it is always done with a word derived from the Greek root *Paschein* meaning to suffer, the one exception being Col 1.24.[45] This is because his suffering is unlike the suffering of any other, being neither sin pain nor human pain. We are told that he was born of a virgin after the Holy Spirit came upon her, the link between pain and suffering through simply being born with a sinful nature was not in place. Through his life he endured the temptations that are common to us all, not falling once. In the face of his accusers no one could lay a charge of sin against him except that he had upset their beliefs of what a sinless life was. His life was one of continual suffering, born in a stable

---

[45] "Col 1.24 Now I rejoice in what was suffered (*pathema*) for you, and I fill up in my flesh what is still lacking in regard to Christ's afflictions (*thlipsis* = a more general word covering sickness, distress, oppression, tribulation, anguish even birth pains. Here, in reference to Christ's sufferings appears to be used interchangeably with *pathema* and is not meant to convey any other meaning than *pathema*)". Aub Podlich.

and soon a refugee, in his life he was rejected ultimately by all and was executed in a grotesquely painful and shameful way with the full knowledge of the authorities that he was an innocent man

His suffering was the stumbling block for many. The Jews said that because he suffered he could not be God, while the Gnostics taught that because he was God he could not have suffered.

Here there is no more blatant case of undeserved suffering and it is here that the charge against the goodness and justice of God must be levelled. So heinous was the crime that creation itself revolted, the ground split, the sun refused to shine and the veil of the temple tore from top to bottom. When evil men looked on and mocked, why was God silent? Because it was God Himself in the form of the Son, nailed to that cross. This occurred, not through some misguided scheme of the priests but through the predeterminate wisdom and foreknowledge of God, Acts 2:23. Through the blood and anguish of this suffering came the salvation of many.

THE SUFFERING OF PEOPLE

The same word is generally used for Christians suffering as is used for Christ's but while non believers can receive all manner of hardship and sickness (*thlipsis*) they, with three exceptions,[46] do

---

[46] These references are to Pilate's wife Mt 27:19, the bleeding Woman, Mk 5:26, and the Galileans killed by Pilate. The link is still present with the special meaning of *paschein* for Pilate's wife suffered because of Him, while the Galileans were killed while at worship and is used in the contest of persecution.

not *paschein*. Other words used of Christian suffering are *Thlipsis, Atimadzo* and *Kakoucheo*. The first word mentioned is also used of Christ's suffering and while a general term for the world's suffering can also be used of the specific suffering of the Christian, e.g. 2 cor 1:5-8 (where the term used is clearly interchangeable with *paschein)* and Rom 5:3.   *Atimadzo,* Acts 5:41, and *Kakoucheo,* Heb 13:3, are both used once and refer to specific types of *paschein* and mean dishonour, treat shamefully and maltreat or torment respectively.

This suffering must be differentiated from the suffering that is common to all in four different ways. These are;

Firstly. Suffering for Christ is inseparable to being in the kingdom, the one giving evidence to the other, Rev 1:9; 2 Tim 1:8; Acts 9:16; 2 Thess 1:5; Rom 8:17; Phil 3:10; 2 Tim 3:10-12. Christ's command to his disciples was to take up his cross daily to follow him. This "kingdom suffering is "given" and "received". It is almost treated as if it is a promise given by grace itself". Importantly sickness is never spoken of in this way.

Secondly. The pains and the joys of the kingdom are one, Heb 12:2; Acts 5:41; Rom 5:3; I Thess 1:6; 1 pet 3:14; Col 1:24; 1 Pet 3:14. This joy is not spoken of in the face of general suffering which the ungodly as well as the godly experience but is linked to suffering for Christ.

The bleeding woman suffered a great deal at the hands of others this is not the suffering of sickness but akin to persecution.

Thirdly. The present pain is always far outweighed by future glory, Rom 8:18; Acts 24.26; Acts 17:24-25; Eph 3:13; 1 Pet 1:11, 4:13, 5:1. This connection between suffering and glory is only present when it is suffering for Christ's kingdom. There is no New Testament connection between sickness and glory.

Fourthly, Suffering for the kingdom is directly linked to the will of God 1 Pet 2:20, 3:17, 3:14, 4:15-16, 5:10. Never does the New Testament say that we are called to pain or suffering outside of the kingdom but inside the kingdom it is God's will that we suffer for him.

Kingdom pain is completely different from human pain. Human pain befalls the good and bad alike and comes because of our own humanity. The faith with which it should be met can deeply enrich the life of a Christian and likewise those who must watch. The suffering itself is neutral and carries no merit for enduring it. Kingdom pain for its part it comes not as a consequence of our human nature but from God's approval of our regenerate nature, Acts 5:41, as it strives to please its maker, 2 Tim 3:12. When met with faith, that faith strengthens the church, 2 Tim 2:10, and carries great reward, perhaps in this world, 2 Tim 3:11, certainly in the next, 2 Tim 2:12, and so is a cause for rejoicing.

The counsellor must determine if the suffering the questioner is experiencing is because of or in spite of God's kingdom. If it is for God's kingdom he must direct him to the will of God and the joys and glory that can be his when he humbles himself under God's powerful hand. Kingdom suffering must be seen as originating in the love of God and an outworking of the regard and confidence He has in the recipient. Far from designed to ultimately crush the believer it must be seen as forming more completely the image of Christ in him.

A BIBLICAL EXPECTATION

At the time of Christ the Jewish world was looking for the *eschaton*. This they believed would be the climactic end to this age with all its pain, suffering, injustice and humility. It was a time when God would step into the course of history, roll it up like a worn carpet and renew his creation. They believed they were living on the very brink of history. The Jewish eschatological hope is illustrated below

The Jewish Eschatological Hope[47]

The Eschaton

This age	The age to come
Sin	Righteousness
Sickness	Health
Demon possession	Health
Evil men triumph	Spirit triumphs

---

[47] Fee, G.D. *Corinthians, A Study Guide.* (ICI: Brussels, 1979) 84.

With the preaching of the coming Messiah by John the Baptist, the Old Testament church had come to a fever pitch in its expectation of the *eschaton*. The disciples all believed that their rabbi would usher in this glorious day. But then Jesus, the mighty Messiah was crucified in the greatest exhibit of weakness that the world has ever seen. The devastation of the disciple was soon replaced with elation when, three days later, Jesus confirmed his power by rising from the dead. Surely, they thought, he would usher in the *eschaton*, Acts 2:6. Instead of the world coming to a climactic end Jesus returned to his Father and the Spirit was given. The church was forced to reconcile a world in which the Spirit worked in power through signs and wonders, a sign of the new age that had dawned, and the continuing existence of the old age that had clearly not passed away. Peter, in his sermon in Acts 3 shows that they had come to realize that Jesus did not come to bring the *final* end but rather the *beginning* of the end. "The blessings of the future had already come. But in another sense, the end had not fully come. Thus it was *already*, but *not yet*."[48] The Christians, like the Jews, saw themselves as eschatological people living between the beginning of the end and the consummation of the end. The following time line illustrates the Christian Eschatological hope

The Christian Eschatological Hope[49]

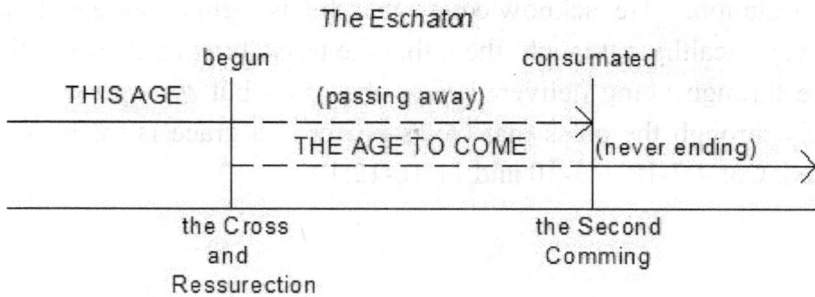

The Eschaton

```
              begun                    consumated
  THIS AGE         │   (passing away)
  ─────────────────┼ ─ ─ ─ ─ ─ ─ ─ ─ ─ →
                   │   THE AGE TO COME      │(never ending)
                   ├ ─ ─ ─ ─ ─ ─ ─ ─ ─ ─ ┼              →
  ─────────────────┴─────────────────────┴─────────────────
           the Cross                 the Second
             and                      Comming
         Ressurection
```

To be a Christian means to live in tension with your environment. We are *already* forgiven but not *yet* perfected, Phil 3:7:14, have *already* experienced a death, 1 Cor 3:22, *yet* will still die, *already* living in the spirit *yet* in a world controlled by Satan, *already* justified and free of condemnation, Rom 8:1, *yet* face a future judgement, 2 Cor 5:10. Unfortunately, many, faced with this tension, cannot hold to a true Christian eschatological hope. Some hold to a *not yet* eschatology and see all their blessings being received in a coming age and expect very little from God for the present. Suffering is born stoically and with the appearance of faith but is an impoverished shell of the reality. The other area, the one we see in the Corinthian church, is what has been called an over realised eschatology. This view holds that the only glorious church is one in which signs and wonders are continually evident and, because God heals, he must heal everybody who calls on him in faith. This view holds little place for weakness and suffering and the true spiritual life is one lived in a frenzy of manifested spiritual gifts.

---

[49] Fee *Corinthians..*, 85.

The Corinthian Church had rejected Paul because he did not fit their view of a spiritual man, let alone an apostle of the mighty God. Much in Paul's letters to them corrects this wrong expectation. He acknowledges that he is neither eloquent nor always healthy but taught them that the true Christian does not find life through being delivered *from* the cross but *through* it. It is only through the cross that God's power and grace is manifested, see 2 Cor 4:7-18, 6:3-10 and 11:16-12:10.

The counsellor must be quick to distinguish between great faith and the resolve of the Stoic and give counsel correcting a faulty eschatological view that leads to the conclusion that pain and suffering, not rich blessing, is all that can be expected in this world. Pain can also be very hard born because of an equally faulty eschatology where the Christian life is seen as one of glory and not of the way of the cross. The counsellor must also gently correct those whose faulty eschatology has caused them to expect only a life of blessings that is not yet theirs. In his pastoral roll the counsellor must prepare his flock by teaching them to live in the tension of the already, but not yet of God's blessings.

4. A THEODICY

INTRODUCTION

The word *theodicy* is derived from two Greek words *theos* (god) and *dike* (justice) and was coined by Leibniz in 1710 when he wrote a very significant work on the problem called *Theodicy*. A theodicy deals with more than the problem of sin for there is much evil in the world that is not sinful. Evil is described as the destruction of the good and can equally be the result of a natural disaster or an accident, as it can be the result of someone's sinful actions. If there is no answer to the problem of evil we are left with either a God who does not exist or who is an omnipotent fiend. "The purpose of all theodicies is to show that regardless of the sufferings, tragedies, mysteries, evils, enigmas, puzzles and catastrophes that beset the universe and particularly man, God's rule is nevertheless holy, wise, good and just."[50]

By its very nature, the problem of evil cannot be totally separated from philosophical considerations. These by their very nature, not being grounded in revelation, must fall short of a satisfactory answer. As many philosophical answers have been coupled with scripture and presented as answers to our questioner's dilemma we must look at some of the most important answers and see their deficiency before moving to a Biblical theodicy. The failing of many of the deficient answers is that they present a *response* to evil as the *answer* but this is ultimately avoiding the issue. It is important to understand that many standard answers are more from the world of philosophy than the Scriptures or so intermingled that

---

[50] Ramm *Christian...*, 121.

it is difficult at first glance to sort the truth from its accretions.

UNSATISFACTORY ANSWERS

GOD'S WAYS ARE DIFFERENT FROM OUR WAYS

There is no doubt that God's goodness is different from our own, While man in his total depravity is incapable of making absolute judgements about goodness, how different is God's goodness to ours. As a person strives to become a truly good man from previously being a sinner, there is a distinct change in what he terms good, but this change is not a reversal but rather a broadening of what he termed previously "good" in a direction he would call "better". "Divine "goodness" differs from ours, but it is not sheerly different: it differs from ours not as white from black but as a perfect circle from a child's attempt to draw a wheel".[51] God's image, though flawed, is still present in man

If God's goodness is essentially different from ours, the call to repentance would have no validity, rather he calls on our own understanding of goodness to judge him, Lk 12:57, Jer 2:5. "If God's moral judgement differs from ours so that our black may be his white, we can mean nothing by calling him good: for to say "God is good" while asserting that his goodness is wholly other than ours, is really only to say "God is we know not what". And an utterly unknown quality in God cannot give us moral grounds for loving or obeying Him."[52]

---

[51] Lewis, C.S. *The Problem of Pain.* (Fontana: London, 1973) 27.

[52] Lewis *Problem...,* 25.

If the counsellor overemphasises the difference between God's goodness and ours, obedience will be based only on fear and not moral grounds and may find that the counsellor and recipient are obeying an omnipotent fiend.

THE DOXOLOGICAL RESPONSE

The Scriptures are clear that the power of Satan is limited and that God is the victor over all that would oppose him. To understand pain and suffering by philosophical means is ultimately of no avail but must be understood through revelation. In the face of suffering, it is said, "the response of the Christian is then that of praise; it is doxological. God has ruled, does rule and will rule. His purposes will not be thwarted. His triumph is assured. God, not evil, has the final word. And therefore Christian man breaks into song in honour, gratitude and praise to the God who is his victor".[53] This view, traditionally that of the Dutch Reformed Calvinists, has been popularised in recent years.[54]

While this is undoubtedly true of kingdom suffering, this teaching is difficult to sustain for human and sin suffering. It is one thing to praise God that an alcoholic, ungodly husband is not beyond his mercy, love and grace but it is an altogether different matter to

---

[53] Ramm *Christian...*,134.

[54] Particularly by Merlin Carothers in his books "Prison to Praise", "Power in Praise", and "Answers to Praise" by Kingsway Publications.

praise God that the father is a sinner and an alcoholic.[55]

The counsellor needs to be aware that this can be a valid response in the face of unjustified suffering but must be aware that this response, in all circumstances, blurs the distinction between sin and righteousness[56] and removes the responsibility of the sinner for his actions.[57] Tragically, the extreme of this doctrine does away with importunate prayer, the very heart of our Lord's prayer.

EVIL CONTRIBUTES TO THE OVERALL GOOD

This theory takes various forms but its overall thrust is that in some mysterious way evil contributes to the overall good in the universe. It is possibly the most common view among Christians. An example of this, called the *aesthetic version*, is the story of a Bishop who had to speak at a mass funeral following a mine disaster in Wales. He held up the back of a tapestry with all its knots and cut threads and pointed out how unintelligible it was but when it was turned around it said "God is love". The thought was that our perspective is wrong and we see only the knots and cut threads, Could we see with God's eyes we would see clearly the pattern of his love.

Though the illustration has merit it does not prove anything,

---

[55] Carothers, M. *Power in Praise* (Kingsway: Eastbourne, 1986) 1-2.

[56] Carothers *Power..*, 5-6.

[57] Carothers *Power..*, 10.

particularly when the theory can be put together in such a way that no checks or objections can be made.

Another variant is the *definition theory* which claims that "only those who have known evil shame, depravity, sin and guilt really understand love, redemption, forgiveness, pardon and salvation."[58] The true saints are those who have struggled with sin and overcome, while the faith of those who have never had this battle is superficial. Certainly the Scriptures teach that those who have been forgiven much should be expected to love much but sin is never presented as the doorway to goodness but a barrier which, but for his grace, would never be crossed. The *struggle theory* teaches that in this battle between good and evil character is formed.

The knowledge of Good and Evil which our forefathers obtained in the garden is never presented as a bad thing[59] throughout the rest of Scriptures. The stumbling block is gaining this information experientially. It should be learned through adherence to God's word and discernment of his prohibitions without the actual expedience of sin.

Calvin's view is called the *instrumental view*. This teaches that evil is never out of control, its presence in the earth being very

---

[58] Ramm *Christian...*, 24-5.

[59] Its absence is seen as the evidence of the immaturity of youth, Dt. 1:35, or the imbecility of age, 2 Sam 19:35, whereas its presence is presented as the gift of a king, 1 King 3:9, the wisdom of angels, 2 Sam 14:17, and ascribed to God himself, Gen 3:5, 22.

restricted and intended for a purpose. "As the foil of God, evil is instrumental in revealing God's glory, his power, his wisdom and his love. If we come across some very baffling cases that seem utterly to defy any attempt to show that they can promote good, Calvin takes refuge in the secret counsels of God".[60]

These different views, though having a large degree of truth to them give little peace of mind in the face of suffering appealing as they do to the unverifiable or the secret counsels of God. They have a place in the counsellor' reply to the problem of suffering but are not the answer in themselves.

THIS IS THE BEST POSSIBLE WORLD

Leibniz, was an accomplished mathematician as well as a theologian and philosopher. "He insisted upon the conformity of the truths of faith to those of philosophy"[61] Using calculus as his model he claimed that God could think of an infinity of possible worlds and chose this world as the best possible world, expressing the maximum amount of good, in keeping with his nature. This good was thought of in terms of compossibility, that is a process whereby many factors, possibly competing, must be weighed off against the other for the best possible combination. This theory took a cosmological view of goodness, i.e. a sufferer must look at the overall picture, not at the amount of pain in his own life. His view in the face of evil was optimism and rationalism, believing as

---

[60] Ramm *Christian...*, 124.

[61] Pelikan, Jaroslav. *From Luther to Kierkegaard*, (Concordia: St Louis, 1963) 87.

he did that behind all evil is an all pervasive good, so much so that he could make evil look like good, losing "its bite, its sting, its agony and appears as part of the great universal scheme of things to promote the goodness and glory of God".[62]   His work had an enormous impact in the study of suffering and since then "most serious studies of the problem of evil deal in some part with Leibniz's solution".[63]

The view of Leibniz must not be dismissed as an obtuse and outdated view of a philosopher. We need to understood it as something that the common man has grasped in times of great national conflict, submitting voluntarily and without questioning to great deprivation, pain and even death. Medical ethics are also closely related to the problem of the greater good. But to understand the necessity for a course of action is far from the same thing as accepting that action as good. This teaching has not passed from our pulpits to this day and is proclaimed in the face of tragedy. by pastors, who have never hear of Leibniz,

Though he raised many issues of merit he strived too hard to "be both a Christian and a philosopher in the solution of the problem of evil".[64] and offered an artificial answer, not recognising "the tension between what must be done and what ought to be done"[65]

---

[62] Ramm *Christian...*, 147.

[63] Ramm *Christian...*, 121.

[64] Pelican *Luther...*, 86.

[65] Pelican *Luther...*,154. It appears that the explanations based on Leibniz's theodicy for an earthquake that occurred on all saints day 1755 killing up to 60,000 people, many while worshiping. This was God's punishment for mans sins "for verily why do people crowd in the slums of big cities when nature wished them to live in her maternal bosom?" The Lisbon earthquake was what

ultimately leaving us with a less than omnipotent God and a "sane account of the insane".

The concept of the overall good has no consolation or answer to the individual sufferer. The value of such arguments by the counsellor has been described as follows; "God himself rejects all false apologias; He will have none of that justification of His domain which his unauthorised pious advocates repeatedly feel obliged to make, a justification that reaches its philosophical zenith in the Theodicee of Leibniz. Such a defence of God by men usually is petty, presumptuous and full of untruths, and convinces only those who want to be convinced at any price. It is, basically, an insult to God".[66]

THE REALITY OF FREEDOM AND EVIL

Man was created in the image of God and even though that image is marred the image is none the less still visible. This image may be interpreted as many things but one of them must be freedom, freedom to choose between good and evil, God or the enemy. Without this freedom he is not in the image of God and while man has this freedom there will always be sin and suffering in the world. The only option for a painless world is for man to become a robot capable of unquestioning and unthinking obedience without

he had to do. This does not explain why the sinners of Lisbon were worse sinners than those in Paris and London. Their destruction then was what he should do. The inconsistency of this arguement was the basis for the revolt against this view.

[66] Ragaz, L. God Himself is the Answer in Nahum N. Glatzer editor *The Dimensions of Job*. (Schocken: New York, 1969) 129.

understanding.

The counsellor should be careful how much he emphasises this aspect. While how much free will a fallen creation has is debatable, certainly that will is completely accountable for the decisions it makes. Also it is certainly through constantly choosing the right that Christian character is formed. But these facts are not an answer to suffering. If it was simply a matter of suffering as a result of a wrong and rebellious choice it would be, but not when it is used to explain how an omnipotent God would allow suffering as a result of someone else's wrong choice. The scripture clearly teaches that there is coming a time when pain and sorrow will pass away along with evil and men will do only the right. It never presents this obedience as coming from automatons.

THE THREE PRONGED ANSWER

INTRODUCTION

This study has been at pain not to minimise the problem of suffering and to present a belief that there are only two ways of viewing it, through unaided reason or the eye of faith. If our understanding is through reason we must agree with Bertrand Russell who, blaspheming God, said "in a world so full of contradictions I cannot find God; I can more easily assume that it was created by a mischievous Mephistopheles in an exceptionally devilish mood."[67] The answers of "faith" as they are sometimes

---

[67] Cited in Oesterley, W.O.E. and T. H. Robinson. The Three Stages of the Book in Nahum N. Glatzer editor *The Dimensions of Job*. (Schocken, New York, 1969) 222.

presented, we have already seen, can have very little to do with a biblical theodicy but seem intended to placate those who will believe anything just to satisfy the deep longing for an answer

The answer, which the writer will present as his theodicy is not profound but in its three pronged answer provides a sufficient answer to the questions raised.

THE SUFFERING OF CHRIST

In our opening page I spoke of the silence of God being the greatest problem in the face of suffering. For two thousand years now he has been silent but this was not always so. There was a time when God was not silent but spoke loudly, his voice thundering down the halls of time and that was at the cross.[68] When we endure suffering these are times of crisis in our lives but, severe and climatic as these may be we need to see them as insignificant compared to the moment of climax of creation. God's son, fulfilling a plan for redemption of his father's creation that was devised before there was even a fall, was crucified by ungodly men. The author of life was murdered, but not by the will of man but the will of the Father himself. Through the shed blood of Christ, sin, no longer covered by animal sacrifices, is nailed to the cross of Christ. The sinner is cleansed, forgiven and shares the same nature and righteousness as the crucified.

---

[68] I have earlier described this as a time when God was silent. Any understanding of the cross involves both these aspects, different things were said in the silence and the shout.

The mystery of lesser sufferings must yield in the face of the greatest suffering and "of all the questions which immediately concern us, there is not one which the cross of Christ has left unanswered. Men point to the sad incidents of life on earth, and they ask, "Where is the love of God?" God points to that cross as the unreserved manifestation of love so inconceivably infinite as to answer every challenge and silence all doubts forever. And that cross is not merely the public proof of what God has accomplished; it is the earnest of all that he has promised".[69]

For the Christian, God's love is not demonstrated by his compliance "with some specific appeal urged in the petulance of present need or sorrow".[70] Rather it is seen in the intensity of Christ's sufferings, which were for us.

CHRIST SUFFERING WITH US

The Almighty has been described as *impassable* from the Latin meaning "without passions"[71] and some have seen in this a God without moral character.[72] The term is generally understood now to refer simply to the belief that God is incapable of being acted on by anything stronger than himself, a confirmation of his omnipotence and perfection. The Godhead, far from being without passion, is consumed with it,[73] The parable of the Prodigal Son

---

[69] Anderson *Silence...*, 150.

[70] Anderson *Silence...*, 150.

[71] E.g. Article 1 of the 39 Articles of the Church of England.

[72] This Platonic view came into the church through the early church fathers.

[73] See Gen 6:6; 1 Sam 15:11, 15:23 (cf. 2 Sam 24.16; Mal 3:6) John 12:23-24, 27-28, 13:31-31, 17:1.

shows the Father rejoicing at the repentance of sinners while suffering on account of the sin of man and his unrequited love to man. There is no consolation in a God who only sympathises with us, We have already mentioned how Christians are often called to suffer with Christ but this is only one side of the picture. True consolation comes when we view the other side of the scene where we see the Lord of Glory who suffers when even the least of those who have put their trust in him, suffer.

This entering into our suffering can be seen also through the ministry of the Holy Spirit who intercedes for us when we are so deeply troubled that we do not know how or what to pray. Far from instructing us, as a school teacher might, he enters right into the intensity of our emotions praying to the Father as we only wished we could, Rom 8:26. Though called to follow Christ and bear the *cross of Christ*, Lk 14:27, (and this can only incorporate "walking in the same way as Christ walked in the humble form of a servant - needy, forsaken, mocked not loving worldliness .... to walk alone)"[74] we have also been called to bear the *yoke of Christ*, Matt 11.30. As the young oxen is yoked to the older experienced animal and the pair share the same burden, so are we to be yoked to Christ.

It was the world that Christ loved and it was for the world he suffered. The suffering of Christ with us must therefore carry with it a logical progression and that is, we share in the sufferings and judgements that befall our community, nation and world. His body

---

[74] Kierkegaard, S. *The Gospel Of Suffering.* (Augsburg: Minneapolis, 1948) 12.

must continue that same love and, as it were, complete the sufferings of Christ. God would "rather risk that the danger of their love may grow cold in the midst of judgements than the much greater danger that in their public preservation they will lose their love for their guilty brothers and sisters who are bought under judgement, and that they finally will proudly say, "I am not as they are".[75] Through this type of suffering the Christian can stand with the impenitent in their time of shame and associate with them and their guilt. Through experiencing the guilt of the community, confession of its sin, Dan 9:3-6, and practical demonstrations of God's love, his kingdom will be advanced.

NOW IS THE TIME OF GRACE

The silence of God over these millennia since the cross requires explanation, for "why does He not use his power to give proof of his goodness, in a way men choose to expect of him."[76] When we ask for God to speak in the face of suffering do we understand what we ask? In the cross "heaven has come down to earth, the climax of Divine revelation has been reached, there is no reserve of mercy yet to be unfolded. He has spoken his last word of love and grace, and when next he breaks silence it will be to let loose judgements that shall engulf a world that has rejected Christ. For our God shall come and not keep silence, Psm 50:3."[77]

When our Lord started his ministry on earth at Nazareth, Lk 4:16-

---

[75]Thielicke H. *Out of the Depths.* (Eerdmans: Grand Rapids, 1962) 49.

[76] Anderson *Silence...*, 161.

[77] Anderson *Silence...*, 149.

22, he read a message of hope from the prophet Isaiah proclaiming deliverance and jubilee to a needy world. Jesus completed his reading halfway through a verse leaving unread "and the day of vengeance of the Lord." While the moral law and its enforcement by society is still in place the judgement of sin is with the Son, for "The Father judgeth no man, but hath committed all judgement unto the Son." He, the judge of sinners is now the sinners saviour.

Till now a great amnesty has been proclaimed, but not to the Jews only, whose covenants were endorsed by public displays of divine power but also to the Gentiles. The response to the preaching of the gospel of grace is the life of faith, the antithesis of walking by sight. This life reserves its greater blessings for those who have believed without having seen, Jn 20:29.

Under the old order, the Father never turned away any penitent, Jew or Gentile, who sought his mercy but Christianity goes far beyond the Law for in it men who did not seek him are actively reconciled to God. Now mercy is not just available to some men but to all. "The era of the reign of grace is precisely the era of the Silence of God. To grace, therefore, we look to explain the silence. Christianity is the supreme and final revelation of the Divine kindness and love towards man. Therefore when God again declares himself it can only be in wrath, and wrath must await "the day of wrath".[78]

We have been dealing with the problem of suffering but the real issue to our society is what it does with its offer of mercy. A man who receives grace at the hand of God and has rejoiced in the

---

[78] Anderson *Silence...*, 164.

amnesty that has been offered to all men, is wrong to cry to God and deny others the same access to that grace that can make the greatest sinner the greatest saint, Much of our New Testament was written by such a man. To cry for God's judgement upon another is to not appreciate the enormity of our own sin and fallen nature and to fail to appreciate that it was for the sins of righteous men and ourselves, not just sinners, that Christ was crucified.

5. CONCLUSION

In addressing the problem of suffering, I have not attempted to give a sane account of the insane. Rather I give the contrary view that the problem of suffering will never be answered by those who approach it with reason and philosophy alone. The unaided mind, though it may boast of its powers can only attain to the Unknown (and unknowable) god of the Greeks, the *Dues Absconditus* of the theologians.

Faith, on the other hand, even when, or perhaps especially when mingled with a heartfelt "Why?" as God's power and his justice appear to diverge, is given consolation in the Scriptures that there will be a convergence of the two themes. There is an answer to the "Why?" of faith but that answer is not a reason but a person, the *Dues Arevelatus,* though this self revelation of God is for some through a period of deep searching and questioning.

There is no promise in Scripture that our suffering will be lightened, only that great suffering can be a light burden. Just as it was possible for the martyrs to sing hymns of praise to an omnipotent and just God as they entered the arena, so we also may still know the lightness of our burden.[79] It is light because we are following him who went before us and the path of suffering has no surprises for our guide. It is light also for it is shared, not by the omnipotent but by the imminent God who has revealed himself and called us to be yoked to him. Our need for justice can be

---

[79] Take, for instance, the hymn "Now thank we all our God, with hearts and hands and voices". It was written by a Lutheran pastor, Martin Rinkart, who, in the middle of the plague during the 30 year war, was burying 50 people a day.

surrendered knowing that we have never received justice at God's hands. An awareness that his hand will not be stayed forever with the coming of his day of wrath must drive us to seek mercy, not wrath, on those who treat us unjustly.

Those who would argue from the world's injustice that a just God cannot exist must give an explanation for the very origin of the belief in a good, just and omnipotent God. Such a belief was more illogical than it is now, arising in a time and society without modern medicine, anaesthetics, surgery, or painkillers and where life could be very short and cheap. Yet in the face of great suffering this belief not only arose but also continue to this day. Such a belief will always continue when men see the answer to "Why?"is really "Who".

BIBLIOGRAPHY

Anderson, R.	*The Silence Of God.* (Pickering & Inglis: London, 9th edition) .
Augustine.	*Confessions.*
Buber, Martin	A God Who Hides His Face in Nahum N. Glatzer editor *The Dimensions of Job.* (Schocken: New York, 1969) P. 56-64.
Carothers, M.	*Power In Praise.* (Kingsway: Eastbourne, 1986).
Fee, G.D.	*Corinthians. A Study Guide.* (ICI: Brussels, 1979).
Glatzer, N. (editor)	*The Dimensions of Job.* (Schocken: New York, 1969).
Hebart, S.P.	*Lutheran Dogmatics.* (Undated lecture notes).
Graham, B.	*Till Armageddon.* (Hodder & Stoughton: Sevenoaks, 1981).
Kierkegaard, S.	*The Gospel of Suffering.* (Augsburg: Minneapolis, 1947).
Lewis, C.S.	*The Problem Of Pain.* (Fontana: London, 1973).
Macgregor, G.	*Introduction To Religious Philosophy.* (Macmillan: London, 1972).
Mc Connell,	*The Promise of Health And Wealth.* (Hodder &Stoughton: Sevenoaks, 1990).

Menzies, W.   *Apologetics.* (ICI: Brussels, 1988).

Oesterley, W.O.E. and T. H. Robinson. The Three Stages of the Book in Nahum N. Glatzer editor *The Dimensions of Job.* (Schocken: New York, 1969) P. 214-224.

Pelikan, J.   *From Luther to Kierkegaard.* (Concordia: St Louis, 1963).

Podlich, A.   Untitled & undated study notes

Pollock, Seton   God and a Heretic in Nahum N. Glatzer editor *The Dimensions of Job.* (Schocken: New York, 1969) P. 268-271.

Ramm, B.   *A Christian Appeal to Reason.* (ICI: Brussels, 1988).

Schmidt, H.   *Doctrinal Theology of the Evangelical Lutheran Church.* Reprint (Augsburg: Minneapolis, 1961).

Schwarz, H   *The Search For God.* (Augsburg: Min. 1975).

Thielicke, H.   *Out of the Depths.* (Eerdmans: Grand Rapids, 1962).

www.ingramcontent.com/pod-product-compliance
Lightning Source LLC
Chambersburg PA
CBHW060052050426
42448CB00011B/2417